You Are a Dirty Old Man
A Joke Book

by

Banis Skip Cloud

DORRANCE PUBLISHING CO., INC.
PITTSBURGH, PENNSYLVANIA 15222

The contents of this work including, but not limited to, the accuracy of events, people, and places depicted; opinions expressed; permission to use previously published materials included; and any advice given or actions advocated are solely the responsibility of the author, who assumes all liability for said work and indemnifies the publisher against any claims stemming from publication of the work.

Dorrance Publishing Co., Inc.
701 Smithfield Street
Pittsburgh, PA 15222
Visit our website at *www.dorrancebookstore.com*

ISBN: 978-1-4349-1309-8
eISBN: 978-1-4349-7052-7

Dedicated to

All the people who have told me a joke. All the people who have enjoyed a joke that I have told. All the people who got the jokes without having them explained to them.

My son and daughters.

My grandchildren.

My great grandchildren.

My friends who encouraged me to write this book.

My X's who I wished were in Texas.

Disclaimer

Mr. Cloud does not take credit for making up the jokes in this book. These are jokes he has heard and told over the years. Jokes are heard and revised and told over the years. So if anyone is offended after reading a joke, find the original author and sue him.

If you are the originator of any of the jokes, let me know and I'll shake your hand and thank you very much.

Some of the jokes in this book have vulgar language in them, but if you try to clean them up they just don't work.

Jokes are ridiculous and should not be taken seriously.

Contents

Three dogs were running along in a desert, one behind the other in single file. The first dog started kicking up sand and it was blowing back in the second and third dogs' eyes. The second dog looked back at the third dog and said, "Ain't that a bitch?" The third dog replied, "By God, it better be."

A man went shopping for an attaché case. As he was going through different cases in a luggage store, he came across an inexpensive case priced at $30. As he progressed, he found a leather one for $75. Then he spotted one for $200 made out of alligator skin. To his surprise, at the end of the assortment, there was one priced at $10,000. Amazed, he called a salesman over to try to get an explanation for the outrageous price. When asked about the $10,000 price tag, the salesman explained that the case was made from the skin of an elephant's penis. The man told the salesman that he could see the novelty of that, but it would not make it worth the price. The salesman explained further that the simple attaché' case when stroked thirty times would turn into a two-suitor; 150 times it would become a large trunk; and 1000 times it would become a minivan.

Q: *What is Pokemon?*
A: Jamaican sex

A little boy and girl were put in the bathtub together for the first time. As they were playing and splashing around, the little girl kept looking between the little boy's legs and looking and looking. Finally, as she points towards his tally, she asks, "Can I play with that?" to which the little boy replies, "Hell, no, I see what you've done to yours."

A little boy and girl were in the swimming pool. As the boy started toward the girl, he says, "I'm going to duck you." The girl replied, "Hell you are, you can't even say it right."

A little boy was taking a leak when the toilet lid fell and smacked his dick. He started crying and hollering for his mom. The mom came and sympathetically asked, "What happened?" The little boy could barely blurt out that the lid had fallen on his wee wee. The mom tried to console him by asking, "Poor baby, where does it hurt?" "Right there," the boy said. "Kiss it, Mommy kiss it!" Disgusted, the mom yells at the boy, "Just like your damn father aren't you?"

Q: *How do you circumcise a red neck?*
A: Put braces on his sister.
Q: *What does oral sex with an eighty-year old woman taste like?*
A: Depends.
Q: *How does a baker man describe sex?*
A: Brownies with nuts.

The neighborhood where I grew up was so shitty they named our street Number "2" Street.

A blind man lived so far out in the country that he didn't have a modern bathroom, so he had an outhouse. He strung a wire from the house to the outhouse and he would hook his cane on the wire to get back and forth. One night, some pranksters took and moved his outhouse six feet further out and reattached the wire. As the blind man was headed out to go, he fell into shit neck deep. He couldn't get out, so he frantically started hollering FIRE! FIRE! His neighbors came running over to help and saw his situation. A bit confused, they asked, "We can understand your emergency but why are you hollering fire?" The blind man replied, "Did you ever hear of anyone getting saved by hollering SHIT?"

As a cop was walking his beat, he came upon a little boy playing beside the road. As he looked closer, he saw the boy was sculpting something out of mud, horseshit, and bullshit. Amused, the cop asked him, "What are you making, son?" The boy replied, "A fireman." *Cute* the cop thought and then he asked, "Why don't you make a police officer?" The boy's quick reply was, "Not enough bullshit."

A veterinarian's daughter went away to college. When she got there, she could only find a room that was a ways from college, so she wrote home to her father to please send some money so she could buy a bicycle. However, by the time the money got there, she found a room close to campus and did not need the bicycle so she bought a pet monkey instead to keep her company. After a couple of weeks the monkey got sick so the daughter wrote to her veterinarian dad and told him that all the hair was falling off her monkey, what should she do. The father writes back, "Sell the bicycle."

A blind man walking past a fish market hollers, "Hello, girls!"

Q: *Did you hear about the new bikini?   -NO-*
A: Two band aids and a cork.
Q: *Did you hear about the dehydrated Frenchman?*
A   Pierre.

Liza and Earldeen were walking down the street when they came upon Leroy. Leroy was showing off his new camera and told Liza and Earldeen to pose in front of the bushes and he would take their pictures. The gals were posing and Leroy was adjusting his lens for the shot. Impatient Earldeen asked Liza, "What is he doing?" Liza's reply was, "He's trying to focus." Earldeen exclaimed, "You mean, 'Bofus'!"

Little Red Riding Hood was walking through the woods when the Big Bad Wolf jumped out from behind a tree and hollered, "Little Red Riding Hood, I'm going to eat you!" to which she replied, "Eat, eat, eat! Doesn't anyone believe in fucking anymore?"

Q: *Did you hear about the new Italian toothpaste?*   -No-
A: Preparation H.
Q: *What happened to the Italian who ran into the wall with a hard on?*
A: He broke his nose.
Q: *Why wasn't Jesus Italian?*
A: They couldn't find three wise men let alone a virgin.
Q: *What do you get an eighty-year-old woman for Christmas?*
A: "Mikey" (He'll eat anything).
Q: *How do you get an eighty-year-old Christian woman to holler "FUCK!" in a crowded room?*
A: In the same room, have another eighty-year old woman holler "BINGO!"

A teenager and his dad were discussing sex for the first time. The teen questioned his dad, "Dad, what does a woman's pussy look like before sex?" The dad thought for a couple of seconds and then replied, "Son, try to imagine a furry rose." "If that's true, Dad," the boy wondered, "what does a woman's pussy look like after sex?" Again, the dad thought a few seconds and replied, "Son, try to imagine a bulldog trying to eat mayonnaise."

Q: *What is an electric fart?*
A: One with juice in it.
Q: *What is a Latin lover?*
A: A fucking Mexican.
Q: *If a big duck can lay a big egg, why can't a little duck lay a big egg?*
A: He hasn't got a big enough Quack.

Last night I thought I was called to preach.   -How's that?-
I woke up with a hard on craving fried chicken.

Back in the old west, an ordinary cowboy walks into a saloon and bellies up to the bar. As he gulps down his first beer, he notices a little dude a little ways down the bar. He scowls at him and laughs. The little dude became very uncomfortable, but he didn't want to seem to be a coward so he ordered a glass of milk and sat sipping it. The cowboy drank a couple more beers and looked at the dude again. "Dude" he says, "Can you dance?" The dude politely said, "No, Sir, I can't." To which the cowboy drew one of his guns and fires at the floor near the dude's feet. The little dude hopped and jumped around to the cowboy's glee and laughter. A few beers later, the cowboy looked at the dude again and said, "Dude are you sure you can't dance?" Again, the dude says, "No, Sir, I can't." To this, the cowboy draws his other gun and fires at the dude's feet. Again, the dude jumped and hopped all over the place. The cowboy laughed and slapped the little dude on the back and says, "Poor little dude." After finishing his last beer, the cowboy staggers out of the saloon and starts to get on his horse. At this point, he hears the click of a hammer being pulled back and feels the barrel of a gun being pressed against his ear. He stops dead in his tracks. The little dude asks the cowboy, "Cowboy, you shot six shots out of that six shooter and you shot six shots out of that six shooter. Have you ever kissed a horse's ass before?" A slight pause, but the cowboy answers back, "No, but I've been wanting to for a long time."

Q: *What did one lesbian frog say to the other lesbian frog?*
A: Hey, we do taste like chicken.

Three gal friends all had boyfriends named Leroy. As they were always getting them mixed up on conversations, they decided to name them after soda pop. The first one comes up with, "I'm going to name mine Seven Up because when he up, he up." The second one decides, "I'm going to name mine Mountain Dew because when he do, he do." The third one pauses and then says, "I'm going to name mine Jack Daniels." The other two objected, "But honey that ain't a soda pop, that's a liquor." The third one proudly chimed back, "That's my Leroy."

Little Red Riding Hood was walking through the woods when the Big Bad Wolf jumps out and hollers, "Little Red Riding Hood, I'm going to fuck you good!" Little Red Riding Hood replies, "Stick to the script you bastard, you're supposed to eat me!"

A new little girl moved into the neighborhood so little Johnny decides to make friends. He approaches her and asks, "What's your name?" Little girl replies, "Mary." Johnny says, "No, no what's your name." She replies, "Mary Jane." Johnny says, "No, no, what's your whole name?" Little girl replies, "Pussy."

A woman was posing nude in front of a full-length mirror. As she was turning looking at herself in different poses, her husband walks in and sees what's going on. He asks, "What are you doing?" She answers, "I went to the doctor today and he told me I had the most beautiful body that he had ever seen." "Is that so," says the husband, "Well, what did he say about your big ass?" The wife quipped back, "Oh, he didn't mention you at all."

Q: *Why does an old dog lick his nuts?*
A: Because he can.
Q: *Why does an old bull wrinkle up his nose when he smells of it.*
A: To make the young ones think it's no good.
Q: *What did Jeffrey Dahmer say to Lorena Bobbitt?*
A: You gonna eat that?

A young Indian boy goes to the tribal chief for answers. "Tell me, Chief, how do Indians get their names?" The chief explains, "When you are born, if we see a horse running across the meadow, we name you Running Horse." The chief continues, "When you are born, if we see the moon rising, we name you Rising Moon." The chief was curious so he says to the boy, "Tell me, Two Dogs Fucking, why do you ask?"

A user was walking down the street when a car hit a man. The man was lying in the middle of the street bleeding and seriously injured. He calls out to the user for help, "Quick, man, call me an ambulance!" "Okay, dude," says the user, "You're an ambulance."

Q: *How many spoiled relationships did Lorena Bobbitt have?*
A: Enough to open up a hot dog stand. Try two
       they're small.
Q: *Why do men's I.Q. go up when they have intercourse?*
A: Because they are plugged into a fucking genius.
Q: *What is the difference between a man and a puppy dog?*
A: Puppy dogs grow up and stop whining
Q: *What is the difference between a woman and*
       government bonds?
A: Government bonds mature.
Q: *What do you have when you have 50 lesbians*
       and 50 lawyers in the same room?
A: 100 people in the same room who don't do dick.

A repairman came to fix Lorena Bobbitt's doorbell. When he asked what was wrong with it, Lorena Bobbitt replied back, "Two dings, no dong."

Q: *Did you hear about the woman sheriff from Texas?*   -No-
A: She had the biggest pose I ever saw.
Q: *What is an Oh No bird?*
A: It's a bird with two-inch legs and a three-inch dick
       and every time he comes in for a landing, he hollers
       Oh, No! Oh, No!

An unemployed lion tamer noticed an ad in the paper that a circus was in need of his services. He went to apply, only to find out the job had been filled by a woman. The owner-ringmaster was so impressed with his resume that he told the lion tamer to be his guest at the show that night and that if the woman tamer didn't work out the job would be his. The ringmaster and tamer were sitting together when the lion show opened. The lions entered the ring, followed by a beautiful, sexy, full-figured blonde woman tamer. The crowd was quiet until the woman tamer cracked her whip a few times and the lions jumped upon the barrels and stood on their haunches pawing at the air. The crowd went wild. The ringmaster looked at the man tamer and asked, "Isn't that great? Do you think you can do that?" The man tamer replied, "Yeah, I can do that." Then the woman tamer cracked her whip and made a motion with her free hand. The lions formed a side-by-side line and started doing barrel rolls over each other. Again, the crowd went wild. The ringmaster, in disbelief at what he was seeing, asked the man tamer, "Look at that! Do you think you can do that?"

The man tamer replied, "Yeah, I can do that!" At this time, one of the lions made a surprise move on the woman tamer and with two quick swats of its paws, it knocked the chair and the whip out of her hands. Snarling with its big teeth showing, the lion started creeping toward the woman tamer. Thinking quickly, the woman tamer pulled off her shorts and lay down spread-eagled. The lion crept up to her, stopped, and started licking her pussy. The crowd went wild. The ringmaster was jubilant and hollered at the man tamer, "I've never seen anything like it! Do you think you can do that?" The man tamer says, "You damn right I can do that! Just get those lions out of the cage!"

Two men were walking past a house when they noticed in a window a nude woman bouncing up and down. They decided to sneak a peak, so they got closer. The woman had a banana sticking in a knothole in the floor and was doing herself with it. "Hey," says one of the guys, "that gives me an idea.

"Tomorrow night, I'm coming back over here and crawl under the house. When she puts the banana in the knot hole, I'll pull it on through and stick my dick up the hole and get some tail." "Sound like a good idea to me," says the other, "Let me know how it works out." A couple days later, the two met again on the street. The guy with the idea was walking bowlegged and in great pain. "What happened to you?" says the other one, "Didn't you carry out your plan with the banana lady? What happened? Didn't your plan work?" "Oh, it worked great, until some son-of—bitch knocked on the door and she tried to kick it underneath the bed."

A woman had to pee so bad that she rushed into the bathroom, sat down with everything showing to her young son who was taking a bath. "What's that?" the boy asked, pointing between her legs. "Oh," says the woman, "that's where the old devil hit me with his hatchet." "Gee," the little boy says, "He got you right in the snatch, didn't he, Ma?"

Q: *How do you make Winnie the Pooh mad?*
A: Stick two fingers in his honey.
Q: *What did the Chinese girl say when she slid down*
        the banister?
A: *Holey Smokey!*

Two old shepherds were training a younger one. After a few weeks out in the middle of nowhere, the younger one was getting very lonely. One night, he asked the two, "Is it true that herders do it with their sheep?" Both replied, "Yep, a man couldn't survive if he didn't." The young one then asked, "How do you do it?" "Well" the older one explained, "You just go down in the middle of the herd and pick one out and mount it. It's as simple as that." The young one asked, "I'm desperate, do you mind if I try?" The other two says, "Not at all, go ahead." The young one went to the herd and picked one out. He grabbed it by the fur on its neck and began pumping the sheep. To his surprise, the older herders began laughing and pointing at him. "What's the matter, am I doing something wrong?" he asked. Through their laughter, the older two replied, "No, but you picked out the ugliest one."

Q: *What did the monkey say when he slid down the flagpole?*
A: Great balls a fire.

When we see a bowlegged man walking down the street, we say, "Look at that bowlegged son-of-a-bitch walking down the street."

Q: *How would Shakespeare put it?*
A: Who doth walk down the path of life with his balls in parentheses?

A man was putting on a condom in the bathroom when his young son walked in. "What are you doing, Dad?" the boy asked.

The father thinks fast and responds quickly, "I'm going to catch a mouse." To which the boy followed up with, "What are you gonna do, Dad, fuck it?"

A woman was having sex with a Frenchman when her husband came home early and caught them. The Frenchman jumped off. Grabbing his clothes, he ran out the door and down the street. The husband grabbed his rifle, aimed, and fired at the Frenchman, shooting his dick off. The Frenchman turned around and stuck his tongue out at him and yelled, "Ha ha ha, you missed!"

A teacher was trying to get her students to take a break and rest a few minutes. She tells her class, "Kids, put down your heads on your desk and rest for a while. If you do, I'll give you all a cookie when you're finished." All the kids put down their heads on their desk right away—except for Johnny.

The teacher tells Johnny, "If you don't put your head down and rest, you won't get a cookie." Johnny replied, "I don't want any of your goddamn cookies!" Shocked, the teacher says, "Johnny, you don't use that kind of language, I won't have it. Now, put you head on your desk or you won't get a cookie." Again, Johnny replies, "I don't want any of your goddamn cookies!" The teacher scorns the little boy, "Johnny, you don't use that kind of language. Now, you go home and bring your mother back here to see me!" Johnny leaves and brings back his mother a short time later.

The mother asks the teacher what was wrong. The teacher tells the mother, "Watch this: Johnny, put your head on your desk and when you have a nice rest I'll give you a cookie." Again, Johnny replies, "I don't want any of your goddamn cookies!" The teacher looks at the mother and says, "See that? That's the problem." To which the mother replies, "Okay, fine, fuck the little bastard, don't give him any goddamn cookies!"

A Mexican walked into a Texas bar and ordered a drink. Hoisting it in a toast, he says, "Here's to the Mexican Eagle with its wings spread wide and great. He flew all the way to Texas just to shit on that lone star state." A big Texan stood up hoisting his drink to a toast and says, "Here's to the state of Texas with its soil so black and rich. Need no terds from your black birds, you Mexican son-of-a-bitch."

Q: *How do you make a woman scream*
  after she has an orgasm?
A: Wipe your dick on her curtains.
Q: *What are the three most dangerous things*
  in the world?
A: A black man with an education, a Mexican with a driver's license, and a Greek with running shoes.
Q: *Who is the most nervous man in the world?*
A: The center on a Greek football team.

A man took his little old aunt to a baseball game. Since she knew nothing about baseball, he was explaining things as the game progressed. A player came up and hit the ball over the fence. The man explained, "That's called a homer and the player gets to circle the bases and scores a run." The aunt seemed to understand. The next player came up and drew a 4-pitch walk. He started walking toward first base. The aunt asked, "Why is he walking toward first base? He didn't even hit the ball." The man explained, "Because he's got four balls." The aunt yells at the player, "Walk proudly son, walk proudly!"

A man and woman were making out and it was getting heated. The man asked the woman, "Can I put it in?" "No" was the woman's reply. It was getting so heated the man pleaded with the woman to let him put it in over and over. The woman kept saying no. Finally, he tells her, "Let me put it in and I'll just put it in a little ways." To this, the woman agrees but she says, "You'll have to promise you'll only put it in a little ways." The man says, "Okay, I promise." He puts it in a little ways, but after a while, it gets to feeling so good he rams it all the way home. After a while, it gets to feeling so good to the woman she yells out, "Go ahead, put it all the way in!" The man quickly responds, "Oh, no, a promise is a promise!"

A husband and wife were driving through Nevada when they were stopped by a state trooper. The trooper went up to the driver's side and asked, "May I see your driver's license?" The wife asked, "What did he say? I can't hear him. What did he say?" The husband answered, "He wants to see my license." The man handed his license to the trooper. The trooper looked at it and asked, "May I see your car registration?" Again, the wife asked, "What did he say, I can't hear him. What did he say?" The husband said, "He wants to see our registration." The husband handed the trooper his registration. The trooper looked at it and said, "From California, huh? The worst piece of ass I ever got was in California." The wife again asked, "What did he say, I can't hear him. What did he say?" The husband answered, "He thinks he knows you from California."

A secretary got bored with every day life, so she decided to make a drastic change. She bought herself a Harley Davidson and outfitted herself in leathers. Off she went to join the Hells Angels. When she got there, they explained that she would have to meet certain criteria to join the group. She said, "Okay, what are the criteria?" The Hells Angel president says, "First, you have to own a hog." She took him out and showed him her new cycle. "Great," he said, "That passes." He then said, "Let me look your garb over." He looked at her all-leather suit, big boots, chains, and Nazi helmet. He said, "Great, that passes." He then asked, "Can you drink?" She led him to the bar where, in a few minutes, she downed 12 shots with beer chasers. He says, "Great, that passes." He thought for a minute and then asked, "Can you curse?" The woman blurted out the most obscene words that ever blistered his ears. The president said, "Passes." He then asked, "Have you ever been picked up by the fuzz?" The woman pondered the question a couple of seconds, then answered, "No, but I've been swung around by the tits."

Q: *What's the difference between a whore and a bitch?*
A: A bitch will fuck everyone but you.

A princess was walking down by the castle's pond when a frog jumped out of the water on to the bank next to her. The frog looked at her and said, "I was once a handsome prince but a witch cast a spell on me and turned me into a frog. If you would kiss me, I will turn back into the handsome prince I was." The princess just looked at the frog without saying a word. The frog again pleaded with her, "It's true I was a handsome prince and if you will kiss me, I will turn back into a prince and marry you. I will bestow you with riches beyond your wildest dreams." As the princess stirred her batter for her gourmet dinner of frog legs, she said, "Yeah, right."

A young girl approaches her mother and asks, "Mom, where do children come from?" The mother replies, "Well, your daddy and I met and fell in love, we got married, and then we went to the bedroom. We kissed and hugged and had sex and that's how you get children." "You mean," the little girl asks, "that daddy puts his penis in your vagina?" "Yes," says the mother, "and that's how you get children." That, night the girl is walking down the hall and peaks into her parents' bedroom. The next morning, she approaches her mother and asks, "Mom, what do you get when Daddy puts his penis in your mouth?" The mother replies, "A new Lexus."

Q: *Who is a guy without a hair on his ass?*
A: One who tries to light farts without any clothes on.
Q: *What do they call a pretty woman in Russia?*
A: A tourist.

Mickey and Minnie are getting a divorce. They are in court in front of the judge. The judge begins, "Mickey, I understand you're suing Minnie for divorce on the grounds of insanity." Mickey replies, "No, your honor. You misunderstood. I didn't say Minnie was insane. I said she was fucking Goofy."

Q: *Why is a man's semen white and his urine yellow?*
A: So he can tell if he's coming or going.

A self-proclaimed lover passed out at a party one night. The other guys decided to play a joke on him. They put an inflatable sex doll beside him on the couch. They left for a while and when they came back, they found the lover awake with a confused look on his face. "What's the matter?" one asked. His reply was, "I guess I fell asleep and when I woke up, there was the most gorgeous girl sitting on my lap." "What happened to her?" another asked. "I don't know," he said, "I started kissing her all over and then I bit her on the ass. She farted and flew out the window and I haven't seen her since."

Down at Disneyland, Snow White was missing. Everyone went looking for her. After hours of searching, they finally found her. Can anyone guess where they found her? She was sitting on Pinocchio's nose, hollering, "Lie, baby, lie! Tell me a big one honey."

A rancher kept catching his daughter screwing the cowboys around his ranch. Finally, he told her if he caught her doing a cowboy one more time, he was going to send her off to boarding school.

The daughter was afraid her dad would carry out his threats so she devised a plan with the cowboys. There was a hole in the barn wall so whenever she wanted some, she would put her bare ass up to the hole and the cowboys would poke her from the other side.

One day, she had just put her ass up to the wall when her dad walked in, "What are you doing?" he asked. Jumping away from the wall, she gave him a quick reply, "Well, Dad, sometimes my butt gets to itching and I put it up to the hole there. The cows lick it and it feels good."

"Okay," the dad believed her.

One day, the old man was out in the barn when his ass started itching real bad. He thought he would try his daughter's solution so he pulled his pants down and put his bare ass on the hole in the barn. A cowboy who saw this from the other side ran up and tried to poke it. The old man hollers out, "Sue Jersey, you've got your horn in my ass!"

Rastus tells Liza, "I can screw you so fast sparks will fly!" Liza says, "Nah, ah." Rastus says, "Come on down to the woods tonight and I'll prove it." Liza agrees but suspicious, she tells her girlfriend, Earldeen. "Y'all come down and hide in the woods and watch in case he pulls something. Earldeen agrees. Meanwhile, Rastus gets a jar and paints it black. He then catches a lot of fireflies and puts them in the jar.

They meet in the woods and Earldeen hides nearby as promised. Rastus mounts Liza and starts pumping at a fairly fast rate. He reaches back and lets a few fireflies out of the jar. Earldeen was shocked, saying to herself, "By golly, it's true!" Rastus picks up his speed, reaches back, and lets some more fireflies out. Earldeen couldn't believe her eyes. "He tells the truth!" Rastus picks up his humping and speed even more. He reaches back but spills the entire jar of fireflies. The fireflies were going everywhere. Earldeen jumps up and hollers, "Liza, Liza get up! Your ass is on fire! Your ass is on fire!"

Two friends meet as they come out of the shower at their club. One looks at the other and says, "I couldn't help but notice you have a cork sticking out of your ass. What's it doing there?" The other replies, "Well, I'll tell you. The other day, I was cleaning out my attic when I came upon this real old dusty bottle with a cork in it. I dusted it off and pulled the cork out. To my surprise, a genie came pouring out. He looked at me and said, "You've freed me and now, I will give you any one wish you desire," to which I said, "No shit."

A man met a sweet young thing who he quickly idolized and fell in love with. After two weeks, they were married. On their honeymoon night, the man thought he would have to teach her everything about sex. So when they got undressed, he pointed to his dick and asked, "What's this, honey?" The gal's reply was, "That's a penis." "No," the man said, "That's a cock." "No, that's a penis," the gal countered. The man became stern and said, "No honey, that's a cock, a cock!" The gal made her point by saying, "Oh, no, that's a penis. A cock is about twelve inches long and black."

Did you hear about the old country boy who thought Ice Hockey was a frozen cow terd?

Q: *When the Pollack got lost in the snow, what did he*
do to get rescued?

A: Waved a white flag.

Two blondes are on the opposite sides of the river. One yells across the river, "How do I get to the other side of the river?" The other yells, "You're on the other side!"

A family doctor and a lady met on the street one day. After exchanging greetings, the doctor asked, "How is your husband, Harold, these days?" The lady responded, "Oh, poor Harold passed away about two months ago." "Oh, I'm sorry," replied the doctor. "What happened, heart attack?" "No," said the lady. "I'll tell you: Harold accidentally ate some dog food a couple of years ago. He liked it so much he wouldn't stop. No matter what I said, he kept eating almost nothing but dog food." "Oh," said the doctor. "Then he died of indigestion or malnutrition because of a diet of dog food?" "No" was the lady's answer, "One night, he was watching TV when Lassie came on. Silly bastard broke his neck trying to lick his balls."

A skunk, a deer, and a giraffe went to a bar and ordered drinks. The bartender served them and then said, "Okay, who's paying?" "Not me," says the skunk, "I spent every last cent I had last night." The deer said, "Well, I had a buck yesterday but I'm broke today." The giraffe looked at the other two and said, "Well, shit fellows, I guess the Hi-balls are on me."

Q: *What is the difference between an Irish wedding*
and an Irish funeral?

A: One less drunk.

Out in the old west, two old men were sitting on the porch of a saloon. Out in the distance, they saw a cloud of dust that kept getting closer and closer. Soon, through the dust, they could see a huge 6'8" three hundred-pound cowboy riding a mountain lion. He was whipping the lion with a rattlesnake. As he stopped in front of the saloon, he reached over and tore a piece of cactus of a plant. He scratched his back with it, rammed it, and went in the saloon. In the saloon, he downed a quart of rotgut whiskey and washed it down with a gallon of beer. He rushed back outside and jumped on the mountain lion. As he started whipping the lion with the rattlesnake, he said, "Partners, I hate to drink and run, but there's a mean son-of-a-bitch chasing me!"

Two men were in a bar when a couple of good looking gals walk by. Eyeing one of the gals, one guy says, "I sure would like to tear that up." The gal hears him and comes over to them and asks the guy, "So you would like to tear me up? Well, come on over to my room because I'm in need." Surprised but willing, the guy goes to her room and quickly gets into the act. He is humping and bumping when the gal reaches over and pulls a feather out of the pillow. She begins flocking him on the head with the feather. "Hey," he asks, "what the hell are you doing?" She replies, "I'm beating your brains out, like you're tearing me up."

I'd take Ginkgo Biloba for my bad memory, but I can't remember to.

New pill developed lately called Ginkgo Viagra. Not only do you get it up but you remember what to do with it.

Wouldn't it be great if they had a reverse Viagra for women that made their pussies smaller?

Two dogs in a phone booth. One said, "Bow"; the other said ,"Wow," and they hung up.

I've got a silver tongue. The other night, I walked into a bar and sat down on a stool next to a good-looking gal. I looked over at her and said, "Do you fuck?" Her reply was, "Not till now, you smooth talking son-of-a-bitch."

Two guys are having drinks at a bar discussing their divorces. One looks at the other and says, "All lawyers are assholes." A fellow sitting a little ways down the bar from them hears this and retorts, "Hey, I resent that remark. I take that as a direct personal insult." The other guy asks, "Why, are you a lawyer?" "No," he says, "I'm an asshole."

A salesman was driving through Texas one day. As he cruised through a desolate area, he saw a young man chasing a jack rabbit. He finally caught it and began fucking it. "Holy shit!" the salesman says out loud, "What kind of state is this?" A little further down the road, he saw an old man sitting on a fence post jacking off: "Damn, what kind of sick state is this?" he says. Needing gas, the salesman stops at the next service station. There, he questions the attendant, "What kind of state do you have here?" "What do you mean?" asks the attendant. The salesman says, "A little ways back, I saw a young man chase a jack rabbit down and rape it. Then a ways further, I saw an old man sitting on a fence post jacking off. Why is that?" The attendant answers with a question, "What, do you expect an old man to chase jack rabbits?"

Q: *Why did they fire the cross-eyed teacher?*
A: Because she couldn't keep her pupils in line.

I once had a girl friend that was different. Her tits were on her back. She wasn't much to look at but she was sure fun to dance with.

A man goes to a bar, sits down, and orders a drink. After he finishes, he lays five dollars on the bar and walks out. The bartender reaches over and snags the five spot and jams it in his pant pocket. As he turns to get a beer for another customer, he sees the owner standing at the end of the bar. The bartender shrugs his shoulder at his boss and says, "How about that silly bastard? He walks out without paying for his drink and leaves a five dollar tip."

A man and his doctor friend were talking about the widow, Mrs. Brown. "Yeah," said the man, "I'd marry her for all her money but I couldn't stand to look at that old ugly face forever."

The doctor says, "You wouldn't have to. Just have sex with her every day for eight weeks and I guarantee it would be too much on a woman her age and she would die." "In other words, screw her to death?" asked the man. "Right," says the doctor, "About eight weeks should do it." Six weeks after the man and widow were married, the doctor went by to see them. As he came down the drive, he saw the old lady out plowing the fields with a team of horses. She was whistling, singing, and dancing around as she worked at a very fast pace. As he got closer to the house, he could see his friend sitting in a rocking chair. He had become gray haired and wrinkled. As the doctor got close to the porch, his friend made a feeble attempt to get up but he couldn't. The doctor asks, "What's happening, did you have sex with her every day as planned?" "'Yes, I did," says the man, "But you couldn't tell the silly old bitch only has a couple of weeks to live, could you?"

A naked woman walks into a bar and ordered a straight shot with a beer back. The bartender says, "Okay fine, but how are you going to pay for it?" the woman throws a leg upon the bar and nods toward her twat, "Will this do?" she asks. The bartender says, "Sure will, but do you have anything smaller?"

Confucius says girl who ride bicycle peddle ass all over town.
Confucius says blonde girl really have black hair by crackey.
Confusias says man who farteth in church must sit in own pew.

Three men were hunting for ducks. One had brought along a dog. "I've never seen a dog worth its weight for duck hunting" one criticizes. "Well, this is a special dog," the owner says, "Here, I'll prove it!" Calling the dog to his side, he instructs it, "Find some ducks." The dog runs off to the other side of some trees and comes back. The owner speaks to the dog, "How many ducks are over there?" The dog barks three times. Sure enough, when the hunters went to where the dog was, there were three ducks. The skeptic says, "That's pretty good, but I need more proof than that." The owner again instructs the dog to find more ducks. The dog runs to the lakeshore line and comes back. "How many ducks are in the lake?" the owner asks. The dog paws the ground ten times. Sure enough, the hunters find ten ducks in the lake. Convinced the dog was special, the skeptic says, "I've got to have that dog. How much do you want for it?" "Not for sale," says the owner, but after the price gets to a figure he can't refuse, he finally sells the dog. The next day, the new owner calls the seller up and demands his money back. "Why, what's wrong?" he asked. "Come out to the pond and I'll show you," the new owner says. They meet and the new owner tells the dog to go find some ducks. The dog runs off and comes back. "How many ducks are there?" he questions. The dog runs over, humps his leg, runs over and gets a stick in his mouth, shakes, and throws it. "See what I mean?" says the new owner, "I want my money back, the damn dog is crazy." The former owner says, "You've just got to learn to read him. He's trying to tell you there's so many fucking ducks out there you could shake a stick at them."

Miss Kitty goes out to the barn to tend to her horse and finds Chester with a big shovel of horseshit and a big hard on sticking out of his pants. "What are you doing, Chester?" she asks. He answers, "Well, you see Miss Kitty, this thang of mine has gotten big and won't go down. Mr. Dillon says to try putting a shovel of horse dunk on it." Miss Kitty pulls her pants off and pulls up her dress. As she lies down in the hay spread eagled, she says, "Never mind that, put it right in here, Chester." Chester exclaims, "You mean the whole shovelful, Miss Kitty?"

"We ate, drank, and made merry until 12 o'clock when merry went home, then we all jumped for joy."

Q: *What does the Catholic Church and K-Mart*
       have in common?
A: They both have little boys' pants half off.
Q: *What is the height of confusion?*
A: Oakland on Fathers' Day.

A man and woman get on a hotel elevator. The man looks at the woman and asks, "Hello, what's your name?" The woman replies, "Janet Smith." Then the man asks, "What are you here in town for?" "I'm here for the Nymphomania's Convention," she says. "Oh," says the man. "That's interesting! I've often wondered who the best lovers are." She says, "It's a coincidence you should ask because we took a vote on that last night and the American Indian came in first." "And who was second?" asked the man. She replied, "The Jewish boys were second. By the way, what is your name?" He quickly replies, "Tonto Goldstein."

Q: *What is the height of conceit?*
A: A flea floating downriver on a leaf on his back
       with a hard on yelling, "Raise the draw bridges!
       Raise the draw bridges!"

A lady goes into a grocery store and as she's shopping, she notices a lot of good looking young men. She starts getting the heat on as it has been a while since she has had sex. She notices a handsome sexy young courtesy clerk at one of the check out so she gets in line. After she is checked out, she asks the young man if he would help her to her car with her groceries. He agrees and starts pushing her cart outside to the parking lot. About the time they hit the edge of the parking lot the lady leans close to the young man and in a low voice says, "I've got an itchy pussy." To which the young man replies, "Look, lady, you'll have to point it out to me. All those Japanese cars look alike to me."

I used to deliver pizzas and ran into some good circumstances from time to time. One night, I delivered one to a house and when the door was opened, there stood a beautiful lady in a lacey teddy. She looked me straight in the eye and as she posed for me, she asked, "What do you think is the most sensuous thing on my body? Wait a minute, I hear someone coming! Step inside!" I followed her suggestion and stepped inside. As she slipped the teddy off letting it fall to the floor, she again asked, "Now, what do you think is the most sensuous thing on my body?" I replied, "Your ears, Ma'am." "What?" she says, "Out of all the beautiful things on my body, you say my ears; why?" I answered, "That was me you heard cumming."

Ray goes into a bar and as he sat there drinking his beer, he noticed a gal come in and sit down by a guy at the other end of the bar. The guy looks at the gal and says, "Tickle your ass with a feather." The gal says, "What?" The guy replies, "Particularly nasty weather." She says, "Why, yes, it has been." This continued with the next couple of gals that came in and sat by this guy. Ray gets curious, so he goes down and asks the guy, "What was all the tickle your ass and weather about?" The guy explains, "Well, when a good looking gal comes and sits by me, I say tickle your ass with a feather. If she smiles, I know I can go further. If she gets offended, I make it sound like I said particularly nasty weather. I get a lot of action this way." Ray says, "Sounds like a good plan to me. Do you mind if I try it?" The guy says, "Not at all. Be my guest." Ray goes back to his place at the bar and sits there drinking his beer. By the time a gal comes in and sits by him, Ray was about ready to fall off his stool. He looks at her and says, "Ahh, stick a feather up your ass?" The gal yells, "What?" Ray quickly says, "Pretty fucking cold, ain't it?"

Q: *What does Kato Kalen's existence prove?*
A: That Ginger and Gilligan did have sex.

If Adam were a black man, there wouldn't be any woman. Why?
He would not be giving up any of his ribs.

An American was taking a vacation in the backcountry of Europe. In a little coastal town, he met up with a little old man. As they began talking, the American asked, "How has life treated you?" Little old man says, "Oh, so-so." "You seem a little dejected," says the American. "Why?" "I'll tell you why," says the old man. "See that bridge over there? I built that bridge. I cut the trees, planed the wood, and nailed every board on that bridge myself. Do they call me McGregor the Bridge Builder, No. And that isn't all," he continued, "You see that ship out in the bay? I built that ship. I cut the trees and planed the wood. Board by board, plank by plank, I nailed it together. Do they call me McGregor the shipbuilder, No. But I go out and fuck one goat."

Q: *How do you have sex with a fat woman?*
A: Roll her in flour and look for the wet spot.

A gal had a tattoo of Merle Haggard on one thigh and one of Box Car Willie on the other. One night at a bar, her boyfriend and his buddy was arguing about which was which. A drunk came walking by and when the two men stopped him, he agreed to help settle their argument. "Now" says the boyfriend "My girl-friend has some tattoos of country western singers and we want you to tell us which is which." "Oh, good" says the drunk, "If there's one thing I know, it's country western singers." The gal pulls up her dress and the drunk stares in. "Well," he says, "I'm pretty sure the one on the left is Merle Haggard and I'm almost positive the one on the right is Box Car Willie, but for damn sure, the one in the middle is Willie Nelson."

I've been jerking off in the shower so much lately every time it rains I get a hard on.

Q: *Why do blondes wear panties?*
A: To keep their ankles warm.

Liza was suing Rastus for divorce. They were in the court-room before Judge Leroy. "Liza," says the judge, "why do you want a divorce from your husband of 30 years, Rastus?" Liza begins, "Well you see your honor, Rastus comes home the other night all liquored up and violates me right in front of my daughter, my mother, and my grandma with pinch nose glasses." Well, you're his wife, he has the right. He has the right," says the judge. "But that ain't all, Your Honor," says Liza ,"then he vio-lated my daughter in front of me, my mother, and my grandma with pinch nose glasses." The judge asks, "Liza, is this his daughter?" Liza says, "Yes, I think so," the judge says, "Well, he has the right. It's his daughter, he has the right." "But that ain't all," says Liza "Then he violated my mother right in front of me, my daughter, and my grandma with pinch nose glasses." "Do your mother live in his house?" asks the judge. "Yes," says Liza. "Does she pay rent?" he asks. "No," says Liza. "Then he has the right. He has the right, he supports her." "But that ain't all," Liza says, "then he violated my grandma with pinch nose glasses in front of me, my daughter, and my mother." "Does your grandma live in his house?" asks the judge. "Yes," says Liza. "Does she pay rent?" he asks. "No," says Liza. The judge says, "Well, he supports her, too, so he has the right, he has the right. "But that ain't all your honor," Liza cries. "Then he takes my grandma's pinch nose glasses and puts them on his violator and say, 'Look around, Big Daddy, see if we miss anybody.'"

Q: *What does a little black boy get for Christmas?*
A: My bicycle.
Q: *What's the difference between a dyke and a rhino?*
A: 25 pounds and a plaid shirt.
Q: *What do you call a Mexican without a car?*
A: Joaquin.
Q: *How do you stop ten large black men from*
      raping a woman?
A: Toss them a basketball.
Q: *What do a Mexican and a cue ball have in common?*
A: The harder you hit them, the more English you get
      out of them.
Q: *How do you say constipated in Chinese?*
A: Hung chow.

During the Iraqi freedom war, it's not too well known but the French did help out. Yeah, really! They taught the Iraqis how to wave white flags.

Q: *How did the US troops break up a bingo game in Iraq?*
A: B-52

The Canadians were going to help out, too. They were going to send two battleships, 6,000 troops, and $500,000 in food, but after the exchange rate, it turned out to be two canoes, six Mounties, and a ham sandwich.

Q: *What's more difficult than getting a pregnant elephant in a Volkswagen?*
A: Getting an elephant pregnant in a Volkswagen.
Q: *How do Italians take showers?*
A: Stand and pee against the wind.
Q: *How do you get a Mexican woman pregnant?*
A: Cum on her shoes and let the flies do the rest.

A traveling salesman was having sex with a married woman when they heard the husband coming home. "Quick, get up in the attic!" The man grabbed his clothes and climbed up in the attic. This was an old unfinished house and as he was rolling around, his balls fell through a crack in the ceiling. The husband came in and looked around. He finally noticed the balls hanging down from the ceiling. "What's that?" he asked his wife. "Oh," she says, "Those are my new china bells." "Do they ring?" ask the husband. "Yes they do," she answers. "All you have to do is tap them." The husband grabs a nearby broom and taps the balls with the handle. "I didn't hear anything," he says. The wife replies, "You have to hit them a little harder, but never mind." "Oh, no," says the husband, "I'm going to hear those suckers ring!" After which, he reared back and hit the balls a hard lick with the broom handle. "I still didn't hear a ring," he says. The wife didn't know what to say, so out came "You have to hit them harder." The husband took both hands and swung and hit the balls as hard as he could. The man in the attic hollers, "Ding, Dong! God damn it, Ding Dong!"

Q: *Why do elephants have four feet?*
A: Because 18 inches just wouldn't do.
Q: *Why do witches take off their panties when they ride their brooms?*
A: Better grip.

A black man walked into a bar with a parrot sitting on his shoulder. The bartender asks, "Hey, where did you get that?" The parrot answers, "Africa."

Q: *What is pink and moist and occasionally smells like pussy?*
A: Look in a mirror and stick your tongue out.

They kicked me out of Boy Scouts. Why?
They caught me eating Brownies.

An old sea captain who had been out to sea for six months came into port. The very first night, he went out and got drunk as a skunk. As drunk as he was, he managed to find a whorehouse. He got the whore in the back room and was humping and bumping when he thought to himself, *Boy, I must be giving this gal the fucking of her life.* Curiously, he asks the gal, "How am I doing, Lassie?" She replied, "You're doing about three nots." "Three nots?" The captain was confused. "Yeah," says the gal, "You're *not* up, you're *not* in, and you're *not* getting your money back."

A woman was in love with two men. One was a plain looking guy who was short and pudgy. The other was a tall dark handsome guy. She decided to marry the one who won a cross-country race. Since the two men were in love with the gal, they agreed to the contest to see who would get her hand in marriage. The two took off running and soon the tall dark handsome guy took a sizeable lead. About 2/3 of the way around the course, the tall guy's dick showed out of the leg of his shorts. It was short and stubby. About this time, the short guy's dick came flopping out of his shorts leg. It was long and huge. The gal, seeing both, hollers out "Cut across, Shorty! Cut across!"

Liza was sitting on her front porch with her legs propped up. Earldeen comes walking by and says, "Liza, honey, put down your legs, I can see you whole rear end." Liza replies, "Shut up and mind your own business, I just paid my rent and I am drying my receipt."

A big dog and little dog were going down an alley when they came upon a garbage can. The big dog knocked it over and ate all he wanted and told the little dog to do the same. The little dog does. They continued down the alley when they came upon a bitch dog. The big dog jumps on her and gets all he wants and tells the little dog to do the same. The little dog does. They went on down the alley until they came to the end. There was a new black Cadillac parked on the street. The big dog went around and pissed on all four tires and told the little dog to do the same. The little dog asks "Why?" To which the big dog answers "Can't eat it. Can't fuck it. Piss on it."

A man goes in a drugstore and tells the pharmacist "Give me a bottle of arsenic." The pharmacist replies, "I can't sell you arsenic." The man says, "Then give me a half bottle of arsenic." The pharmacist says, "I still can't sell you arsenic. What do you want with arsenic?" The man says, "I want to kill my wife." "Why in the world would you want to kill your wife?" asks the pharmacist. To which, the man pulls a picture out of his shirt pocket and upon showing it to the pharmacists, he says, "Look at that ugly bitch!" The pharmacist looks at it and exclaims, "Why didn't you tell me you had a prescription?"

Q: *What do you call two Mexicans playing basketball?*
A: Juan on Juan.
Q: *Why did the blonde co-ed have sex with a Mexican?*
A: Her teacher told her to do an essay.

Back in World War II, a sailor had a leave in a China port. Sometime later, he found he had gonorrhea. He went to the ship's doctor. Upon examining the sailor, the doctor says, "Oh my, this is the worst case I've ever seen! Why didn't you come in sooner?" The sailor says, "I was too embarrassed, but what can you do for me?" The doctor replies, "We'll have to cut it off." "Hell, no!" the sailor yells, "Isn't there some thing else?" "No," says the doctor, "But you can get a second opinion. Go see a Chinese doctor." Thinking he has nothing to lose, he heads to the nearest Chinese doctor's office. The Chinese doctor examines him and says, "Oh, very, very bad. You go to American doctor?" Sailor says, "Yes." "What he say?" asked the doctor. "He says that he'd have to cut it off." To which, the Chinese doctor, disgusted, says, "American doctor always cut, cut, cut. Wait two to three days fall off."

An American was driving through the European backcountry when he came upon a little pub at the edge of a forest. He decided to go in and have a beer. When he got inside, the place was jamming. People were laughing, singing, drinking, and dancing in a party-like atmosphere. All except for one little old man who was sitting off in a corner by himself with his head hung down. The American was curious so he went over and asked him, "Hey, what's wrong? All your friends are happy and joyous and you look so down." "Well, I'll tell you. A couple of weeks ago, Ole's sister got lost in the woods so we formed a search party and searched and searched and finally found Ole's sister. We were so glad we found her that we ate, drank, sang songs, danced, and fucked Ole's sister to the wee hours of the morning." The American shrugs his shoulders and asks "So?" The man continues, "Then, a week ago, Sal's wife got lost in the woods. Again, we formed a search party and looked and looked and looked and when we finally found her, we were so happy that we ate, drank, sang, danced, and fucked Sal's wife to the wee hours of the morning." The American again shrugs his shoulders and says, "There must be more." Whimpering the words, the little man says, "Last night, I got lost in the woods and it's Ole's turn next."

Three old maids went on a picture taking Safari in Africa. A few days into the Safari, they were in camp when a huge gorilla came roaring through camp and scooped up one of the old maids and carried her off to his nest where he physically and sexually molested her until the other two old maids were able to form a rescue party. They were able to rescue her but she was in a semi comatose state, just staring into space and not speaking a word.

The other old maids rushed her back to the States and put her in a hospital. The next morning, the two went to visit her. The victimized maid was lying in bed and still not making a sound and staring into space. One of the other old maids looks at her and says "You poor dear. What an ordeal you must have gone through. What must you be thinking?" She raises herself up in bed a little and says, "The son-of-a-bitch never writes, he never calls!"

A woman was at her gynecologist and in position for her exam. When the doctor went to examine her, he backed off a few feet and exclaims, "Damn, you've got a big pussy!" The woman's embarrassed answer was, "I do not." The doctor says, "Look, lady, I'm in the business and you've got the biggest pussy I have ever seen." After the exam, the woman leaves very upset. She goes home, gets a big mirror, and puts it on the floor. She takes off her clothes and stands straddled legged over it looking down. About this time her husband comes in and inquires, "What are you doing?" The woman replies, "I went to the doctor today and he told me I had the biggest pussy he has ever seen and I'm just trying to see." The husband says, "Okay, but be careful. Don't fall in the big hole in the floor."

A man was walking down the street when he came upon a woman sitting on the steps to her house crying out of control. The man asked her what was wrong and if there was anything he could do. All the hysterical woman could get out was, "Oh, no, Charlie's dead!" She kept repeating, "Oh, no, Charlie's dead!" The man finally gave up trying to help her and continued down the street. A couple of blocks down, another woman was sitting on her car fender crying uncontrollably. The man asked her "What is wrong?" The woman sobbed out, "Oh, no, Charlie's dead, Charlie's dead!" The man found he couldn't console this woman either so he left. While walking on, his curiosity took hold and he decided to go to the morgue. There, he approached the attendant and asked, "Have you got a fellow named Charlie here and why was he so special to the ladies?" The attendant replied, "I shouldn't do this but, yes, we have Charlie here and come on back and I'll show you why he was special to the ladies." He took the man to the back room and pulled the sheets off Charlie, revealing Charlie's huge cock. The man got an instant idea and asked the attendant if he would cut off Charlie's cock so he could play a joke on his wife. For a price the attendant cut off Charlie's cock and gave it to the man. The man went home and sneaked into the bathroom and slips Charlie's cock into his pants. He calls for his wife to come in and as she did so, he unzipped his pants and let the big cock flop out. His wife immediately started crying and hollered, "Oh, no, Charlie's dead!"

An overweight man was reading an ad in the paper that stated "Lose thirty pounds in one session. Guaranteed." The man decided to try it so he went to the weight lost place. He asked an attendant how it works. The attendant replied, "You give me $500 and go into the room with the blue door. Once you're in there, you have to stay; you can't get out." The man agreed and went into the room. Once in, the blue door shuts and locks. Ten seconds later, a gorgeous red head came out of another door with a sign on her that read "If you catch me, you get to fuck me." So the man starts chasing her through an obstacle course and finally catches her whereupon, they made love for at least an hour. When he finally went home, he found he had lost thirty pounds. He keeps thinking about the great sex and decides to go back for another session. This time, the attendant tells him he will have to pay $1000 but he will lose forty pounds, but that would put him below his ideal weight by twenty pounds. The man says he doesn't care, that he can't wait for the great sex. The attendant says "Okay" and sends him to a red door. Once inside, the door shuts and locks, and from another door, a beautiful curvy naked blonde comes out with a sign on her that reads "If you catch me you get to fuck me." The obstacle course this time is 15 times as difficult as before. The man chases the blonde and finally catches her and they had sex for hours. When the man finally drags himself home, he found he had lost forty pounds. He was twenty pounds underweight. The man keeps thinking about the great sex and couldn't keep himself from going back for another session. The attendant strongly advised him not to go for a third session but the man was obsessed with the sex and demanded to go in the third room. The attendant finally agreed but warned him of the extremities of the room with the black door and that he could lose fifty pounds or more. The man said he didn't care. He went through the black door and it closed and locked. From another door, out jump a huge gorilla with fire in his eyes and snot coming from his nose. His sign read, "If I catch you, I get to fuck you."

Q: *What is the pickup line in Martinez?*
A: Nice tooth.
Q: *What is the difference between garbage and Arkansas women?*
A: Garbage gets taken out once a week.
Q: *What college did Michael Jackson go to?*
A: Bring 'em young.
Q: *What did the woman on the beach say to Michael Jackson?*
A: Hey, you're in my sun.
Q: *What does Sadaam Husein and Michael Jackson have in common?*
A: They were both found in small holes.
Q: *Why do black people always have chickens?*
A: So their younguns will learn how to walk right.

A guy walks into a bar. He has a normal body but his head was the size of an orange. The bartender looks at him and asks, "What's the story about your small head?" The guy replies, "I was fishing one day and I hooked on to a mermaid and pulled her up on to the beach. She said that if I would let her go, she would grant me one wish. I said okay and asked her how about having intercourse with me." She said that was impossible as she was not equipped for that. She asked if there was some other wish I wanted. I said, "Okay, then, give me a little head."

Q: *What has four legs and one arm?*
A: A happy pit bull.
Q: *How cold was it last night?*
A: My dog woke up and thought he had found a pink Popsicle.
Q: *How was copper wire invented?*
A: Two Jews fighting over a penny.
Q: *Why don't black people listen to country music?*
A: When they hear hoe down they think one of their sisters has been shot.
Q: *Why did God give black men long dongs?*
A: To make up for putting pubic hair on top of their heads.

Q: *Have you heard about the new men's hygiene spray?*
A: It's called umpire for foul balls.
Q: *What do Whitney Houston and Michael Jackson have in common?*
A: They both have twelve-year old crack habits.

George W. Bush and Laura were having trouble getting excited about sex. George W. had always heard that Bubba Smith was a womanizer and had a great reputation in bed. So George W. called Bubba and told him about his problem and asked if he had any suggestions or ideas that might help. Bubba told him to go take a long warm shower, come running out of the bathroom soaking wet, and holler, "Whuff! Whuff!" then jump upon the bed and hit his dick on the bedpost four times. George W. says, "I don't know. Do you think that would work?" Bubba says, "It works for me." So George W. gets in late that night and Laura is already in bed. He goes in and takes a long warm shower, comes running out of the bathroom soaking wet, hollers "Whuff! Whuff!" jumps up on the bed and hit's the bedpost with his dick four times. Laura rolls over all excited and yells out "Is that you Bubba?"

Q: *What do you call a smart blonde?*
A: A Labrador.
Q: *What do you call a blonde with two brain cells?*
A: Pregnant.
Q: *Why did they make aspirin white?*
A: They wanted them to work.
Q: *What do you see when the Pillsbury Dough Boy bends over?*
A: Doughnuts.
Q: *Why did O.J. move to Alabama?*
A: Everybody's D.N.A. is the same.

A widowed man gets himself a new girlfriend but she wouldn't become intimate unless he used a condom. So he goes to the drugstore and asks the pharmacist for a box of condoms. The pharmacist asks, "What size?" The man replies, "Hell, I don't know, I haven't bought condoms in years." The pharmacist tells him to go back to aisle four and see Maria. The man goes and sees Maria and tells her he needs to know what size condom he needs.

Maria unzips his pants and fondles him a little and says, "You need a large. Tell the pharmacist you need a large." So he does.

Same thing with a recently divorced man. His new girlfriend wouldn't have sex unless he used a condom so he goes to the drugstore and asks the pharmacist for a box of condoms. The pharmacist asks, "What size?" The man replies, "Hell I don't know, I haven't bought condoms in years." The pharmacist tells him to go back to aisle four and see Maria. The man goes to Maria and again, she unzips his pants and fondles him and tells him to tell the pharmacist he needs a medium.

A teenage boy has a hot date for Saturday night and he thinks he better have some condoms just in case. He goes to the drugstore and asks the pharmacist for a box of condoms. The pharmacist asks, "What size?" The teen replies, "Hell I don't know, I haven't ever bought condoms." The pharmacist tells him to go see Maria on aisle four. The teen goes to aisle four and tells Maria he needs to know what size condoms he needs. Maria unzips his pants and starts fondling him. A few seconds later, a voice comes over the store speakers: "Clean up on aisle four."

A man picked up a stick of dynamite and it went off blowing his complete left side off. He's all right now.

A blonde and a brunette were sitting in a bar. There was a good-looking man sitting at the other end. The brunette says, "That guy down there is sure good looking but he needs Head and Shoulders." The blonde asks, "How do you give shoulders?"

Q: *What do you get when you cross a goat with a black man?*
A: A weed eater that doesn't work.
Q: *Why do women have two sets of lips?*
A: So they can piss and moan at the same time.
Q: *What do you get when you stand a blonde on her head?*
A: A brunette with very bad breath.
Q: *What do you say to a redneck in court?*

A: Will the defendant please rise.

Q: *What is the difference between a battery and a woman?*

A: The battery has a positive side.

Q: *What is total confusion?*

A: A blind lesbian on a tuna boat.

Q: *What do you call a dog with no hind legs and steel balls?*

A: Sparky.

Q: *What does Michael Jackson like about twenty-six-year olds?*

A: That there are twenty of them.

Q: *What's the difference between Saint Patrick's Day and Martin Luther King Day?*

A: On Saint Patrick's Day, every one wants to be Irish.

Q: *What separates the men from the boys in Greece?*

A: A crow bar.

Q: *What do you call a Ukrainian who's been thrown out of bars?*

A: A bounced check.

An 85-year-old blind man went to Victoria Secret to buy his 80-year-old wife a birthday present. A saleslady helped him pick out a real nice teddy that cost $600. The old man took it home and surprised his wife with it. She went upstairs to put it on for him but it was too small. She couldn't get it on. Not wanting to disappoint him, she decided to go downstairs naked. When she got downstairs, she remarked, "Oh, honey, I love it, come here and give me a hug." The old man went over and put his arms around her and ran his hands up and down her back, "Damn," he says "For $600 you would think they would at least iron it."

Q: *What is a redneck?*

A: A man who drives the same car he was conceived in.

A supply salesman went to Las Vegas and on his very first sales call, he made a huge sale. That night he was having a drink at a bar when he decided he should celebrate. He asked the bartender if he knew any hookers. The bartender said yes and made a phone call to arrange a date at the man's room at 8 p.m. At 8 p.m., a knock came on the man's hotel room door and in came a beautiful blonde. The blonde asked what he would like. Aware and worried about AIDS and disease, the man answered, "How about a hand job, and what do you charge?" The blonde replied, "$500." The man exclaimed, "$500 for a hand job!" The blonde took him over to the window and pointed out and said, "You see that mini mart gas station over there and that fine restaurant over here? I bought all those with hand jobs." Impressed, the man agreed to the price. He was glad he did because it turned out to be a great hand job.

The next day, the salesman went on another sales call and made even a bigger sale than the day before. Wanting to celebrate again, he approached the same bartender and because the hand job had been so great, he asked him if he could get the same blonde. The bartender made the call and again the blonde was to come at 8 p.m.

Once inside the room ,the blonde asked the man what he would like. The man replied that the hand job was unbelievable but he wanted to go a step further and get a blowjob and how much would it be. The blonde replied "$2000." The man was floored. "$2000 for a blowjob? That's unreal." The blonde led him over to the window and pointed out, "You see that High Rise Office building over there and the Hotel Casino over there and that Mega Shopping Center over there? I bought those with blow jobs."

Impressed, the man agreed to the price and was overwhelmed by how great the sex act was.

The next day, the salesman went on another sales call and made a monstrous sale bigger than both previous days sales combined. Again, he wanted to celebrate and because he couldn't get the previous sex acts out of his mind, he went to see if he could hook up with the same blonde—again, through the bartender. The bartender made the call and the blonde showed up at the hotel room again and asked what he would like. Very excitedly, the man replied, "Well, the hand job was terrific and the blow job was so incredible that I just have to have the pussy!" To which the blonde replied, "Pussy! Pussy! If I had one of those, I'd own this fucking town!"

A hillbilly decided to go to the county fair and try to buy some pigs so he could become a pig farmer in order to have meat for his family. When he got to the fair, he approached a man who had pigs for sale but the man told him he only had six sows and no boars. The hillbilly asked how he was to raise pigs without a boar. The seller told him he'd just have to do it himself.

The hillbilly asked how he could tell if it had taken. The seller said if the pigs were wollering in the mud the next morning, it had taken. So the hillbilly loaded the six pigs in his truck and on the way home, he stopped in the woods and did all six pigs. He took them home and the next morning, he looked out the window but the pigs were not wollering in the mud. So he loaded the six pigs in the truck and took them to the woods and did all six again. He took them home and the next morning, he looked out the window but the pigs were not wollering in the mud. Again he loaded all six pigs in his truck and took them to the woods and did them all again. He took them home and the next morning the man was so tired he couldn't get out of bed so he told his wife to go to the window to see what the pigs were doing. When his wife got to the window, he asked her, "What are they doing, are they wollering in the mud?" The wife replies, "No but all six of them are in the truck and one of them is honking the horn."

The organ player is playing and the congregation is singing in a rigorous manner when from the back of the church, a voice rings out, "The organ player is a mother fucker." The preacher throws up his hands and hollers, "Hold it! Hold it! I want to know who calls the organ player a mother fucker." All was quiet; nobody would admit to it. "Okay," says the preacher, "Let's not have any more of it. Let's sing and praise the Lord, play on, organ player." About the time everyone was back into it, another voice from the back came ringing out, "The organ player is a mother fucker." Again, the preacher throws his hands up and hollers, "Hold it! Hold it!" The music stops and the preacher says in stern words, "I want to know who calls the organ player a mother fucker." Not a sound could be heard, nobody would admit to it. "Okay" says the preacher, "No more mother fuckers. Am I understood? Let's continue. Play on organ player." The music begins and the singing is loud and robust. But about this time, another voice squeaks out, "I want to know who called that mother fucker an organ player!" The music and singing stops and the entire congregation shouts out, "That's right! That's right!" The preacher throws up his hands and says, "Okay, I be cool, I be cool! Play on, mother fucker."

A little old lady was walking her little dog when out of nowhere, a big mangy dog jumped the little dog and got hung up. The lady was frantic and hollered, "Shoo, big dog, shoo!" But the big dog kept on pumping. About this time, a little boy was coming down the sidewalk with a broomstick in his hand. The little lady called to the little boy, "Little boy, help me get this big dog off my little dog!" The boy replied, "I don't know if I can. If it's old Spot, I can." The lady says, "Please try. I'll give you $20 if you can get him off." The little boy said, "I don't know if I can, if it's old Spot, I can." The lady said, "Please, try." The little boy said, "Okay, I'll try." So he took the broom handle and poked it in the big dog's ass. He poked it in and out a few times and the big dog yelped, jumped off, and went running down the street. The little boy said, "Yep, that's old Spot all right. Old son-of-a-bitch can dish it out, but he can't take it."

Back in the pirates' days, a man was sitting on the docks watching a ship being unloaded. Just then, he saw a pirate coming down the dock with a peg for a leg, a hook for an arm, and a patch over one eye. Curious, the man went up to the pirate and asked how he had lost a leg, an arm, and an eye. The pirate told him, "I lost me leg in a battle between two ships when a cannon ball hit next to me, tearing it off and that's how I lost me leg." The man then asked, "And how about your hook, how did that happen?" "Well," the pirate said "A couple of years later, I was in a fierce hand to hand battle with some other pirates who was trying to take our loot. Then one of them scored a lucky whack with his sword and cut it almost all the way off. That's how I lost me arm and got me hook." The man asked the last question, "How about the eye, how did you lose the eye?" The pirate continued, "Well, one day I was out on deck and I looked up and a seagull was flying over and shit right directly into me eye." The man asked, "I can understand that being uncomfortable but how did that put out your eye?" The pirate replied, "Twas the day after I got me hook."

Q: *What is the last thing a China man sees as he exits the freeway in his car?*
A: Another driver's middle finger.

A bear is out in the forest when all of a sudden a hunter appears and shoots at the bear, grazing his arm. The bear runs up to the hunter and slaps the gun out of his hands. He yells at the hunter, "Why are you hunting us bears for? We never did anything to you. Just for shooting at me you're going to give me a hand job." The hunter says, "Well, ah." The bear hollers at him, "If you don't I'm going to kill you." So the hunter gives the bear a hand job and starts to leave. The bear warns the hunter, "And don't be coming back hunting us bears anymore." The next morning, the hunter comes back and shoots at the bear again, missing him by at least ten yards. The bear runs up and slaps the gun out of the hunter's hands and again yells at him, "Why are you here shooting at us bears? Why are you hunting us bears? Just for that, you have to give me a blow job." The hunter says, "Well, ahh." The bear yells at him, "If you don't, I'm going to kill you." So the hunter gives the bear a blowjob and starts to leave. The bear warns him, "Don't come back hunting us bears. You won't believe what will happen to you." The next morning, the bear is in the woods and to his surprise, the hunter appears and fires his rifle in the air. The bear runs up and slaps the gun out of his hands. The angry bear gets right in the hunter's face and yells, "I told you not to come back hunting us bears. Now I'm going to butt fuck you." The hunter says, "Well, ahhh." The bear threatens him again, "If you don't, I'm going to kill you." The hunter gets down on his hands and knees and the bear butt fucks him until he is completely exhausted and sprawled out on the ground. The bear tells him, "Now get the hell out of here and don't come back hunting us bears. You won't believe what will happen to you if you do." The next morning, the hunter appears in the woods and stands looking at the bear with his gun at his side. The bear runs up, slaps the gun aside and looks the hunter in the eyes and asks, "You're not here for the hunting, are you?"

After a shipwreck, a man was stranded on an island with six beautiful women. He could not have been more pleased. During the day, he would hunt, fish, and gather food for them. At night, he would have sex with all six women. After a while, he found himself super tired so he cut down on the sex by doing three every other night, but this was really taking a toll on him so he decided to have sex six nights a week and take Sundays off to rest. But with the gathering of food and providing shelter and having sex six nights a week, he was completely exhausted. One morning, he saw a raft washing ashore and on it was a man. He shouted, "Hooray" knowing that he would finally have some help. He ran to the raft and pulled the man up on to the beach and excitedly exclaim, "Man, am I glad to see you!" The other man says sweetly, "Man, I'm glad to see you, too, sweet cheeks, 'cause I'm in need." All the man could think of at this point was, "Ah, shit, there goes my Sundays off!"

Three brothers were talking at their High School reunion. One started by bragging, "Did you know of a machine process that converts seawater to freshwater? Well, I invented that and am president of a large company." The second one bragged, "I invented a scope that allows doctors to operate without cutting the patient wide open. I am the CEO of a large company." The third brother asked, "Well, did you hear of gonorrhea?" The two others quipped back, "Don't tell us you invented gonorrhea?" "No," says the third man, "But it is I who am the West Coast distributor."

A young boy goes into a whorehouse. The madam meets him at the front and tells him, "You're too young to come in here." Flashing a wad of bills, the young boy offers, "I have lots of money and am willing to pay your price." The madam looks at the money and says, "Okay, you got the money all right. Come on in and make your choice of girls." She lines up her girls and the boy immediately picks one. The madam tries to change his mind, "Why did you pick her? She is not the prettiest and she's overweight and besides that, she has V.D." "All right," the boy shouts, "That's what I thought and that's what I wanted." "But why?" the madam asks, "You want to get V.D.?" "Well, I'll tell you," the boy says, "I'll take it home and give it to my sister, my sister will give it to my dad, my dad will give it to my mom, and my mom will give it to the mail man. I'm after that bastard's ass. He kicked my dog."

An American couple was heading to Mexico for vacation when they stopped at the border crossing. The guard exchanged pleasantries with them and asked, "Where are you going in Mexico?" To which the husband replied, "Juarez." The guard became protective of them saying, "Oh, no, Señor, you don't want to go to Juarez. Speedy Gonzales lives in Juarez. He'll fuck your wife just like that," snapping his fingers. The couple continued on and down the road, they stopped at a little Café and during conversation with the waiter. He, too, asked, "Where are you folks going?" "Juarez" the man replied. "Oh, no," the waiter says, "You don't want to go to Juarez. Speedy Gonzales lives in Juarez. He'll fuck your wife just like that." Concerned, but since they had non-refundable reservations, they decided to continue on to Juarez. When they got to Juarez, they were checking into the hotel when the clerk ask, "Señor, you have such a beautiful wife, why do you bring her to Juarez? Speedy Gonzales lives here. He'll fuck your wife just like that." That night as they were in bed and starting to go to sleep, the man's concerns increased so he took preventive measures by putting an index finger in each of his wife's holes. Out of nowhere came a sneeze and without thinking, he took his right hand up to cover the sneeze. Realizing what he had done, he quickly shoved his finger back down in the hole. He was startled by a little voice, "Pardon me, Señor, but you have your finger in my asshole."

Just a little Thursday morning humor....

The president, the first lady, and Dick Cheney are flying on Air Force One. George looks at Laura, chuckles and says, "You know, I could throw a $1,000.00 bill out the window right now and make somebody very happy." Laura shrugs her shoulders and says, "Well, I could throw ten $100.00 bills out the window and make 10 people very happy."

Cheney says, "Of course, then, I could throw one-hundred $10.00 bills out the window and make a hundred people very happy."

The pilot rolls his eyes, looks at all of them, and says to his co-pilot, "Such big shots back there...hell, I could throw all of them out the window and make 56 million people very happy."

A teacher starts a new job at a school in San Diego and trying to make a good impression on her first day, explains to her class that she's a Chargers fan. She asks the class to raise their hands if they, too, are Charger fans. Everyone in the class raises their hand except one little girl. The teacher looks at the girl with surprise and says, "Mary, why didn't you raise your hand?"

Because "I'm not a Chargers fan," she replied.

The teacher, still shocked, asks, "Well, if you're not a chargers fan, then who do you support?"

"I'm a Bronco fan, and proud of it," Mary replied.

The teacher could not believe her ears, "Mary, why are you a Bronco fan?"

"Because my mom and dad are from Denver and my mom is a Bronco fan and my dad is a Bronco fan, so I'm a Bronco fan, too!"

"Well," said the teacher, in an obviously annoyed tone, "That's no reason for you to be a Bronco fan. You don't have to be just like your parents all of the time. What if your mom was a prostitute and your dad was a drug addict and a car thief, what would you be then?"

Mary says, "A Raiders fan."

Lightning Source UK Ltd.
Milton Keynes UK
UKHW022131060223
416584UK00024B/482